About the Author

Emelie Sandqvist is a young woman who has just turned twenty years old. She writes to make others feel understood and to remind them that they're not alone in their battles, as everyone has one. She wishes to make an impact on a few, helping their voices be heard and encouraging them to speak up with pride.

Time Does Not Heal All Wounds

Emelie Sandqvist

Time Does Not Heal All Wounds

Vanguard Press

A CIP catalogue record for this title is available from the British Library.

ISBN 978-1-83794-546-7

*Vanguard Press is an imprint of
Pegasus Elliot Mackenzie Publishers Ltd.*
www.pegasuspublishers.com

First Published in 2025

**Vanguard Press
Sheraton House Castle Park
Cambridge England**

Printed & Bound in Great Britain

Dedication

To everyone who feels too much, it is a blessing, not a curse.

the same skin

i know i'm not the skinniest or prettiest,
and i know that i don't have that hourglass body
everyone wants,
or that clean, silk-looking skin

but you held me, you still held me
in a way i thought no one
wanted to
hold me or
touch me

and you looked at me like i meant
the absolute world to you
and for a moment
you treated me like i was the world to you
and i cannot recover from that,
that feeling
that feeling i got when you craved
my skin, my touch
the same skin i so long resented

noticeable

i have already forgotten how
his skin felt against mine
but one thing i cannot forget;
the way he described how he noticed me
i am noticeable
i am noticeable
i am noticeable
and he saw me
i am embarrassed to admit this
but that made me smile while i
kissed him

love myself

i want to be able to say,
"i love myself and the way i look"
and mean it
every single word of that sentence
but i can't
because i don't love my legs and the way they wiggle
when i walk,
i don't love the way my stretch marks on my arms show
when i don't have long sleeves on my shirt,
i don't love the way i always am the laugh on the picture,
because i accidentally made a silly face or my double
chin was showing
i hate it
i hate it
i hate everything with my body at this point

my turn

i feel like it's my turn to be loved
my turn to be picked by guys while we're at a bar
my turn to turn heads while we walk past someone
my turn to be approached by a stranger
my turn to get compliments instead of giving them
my turn to laugh so hard my stomach hurts
my turn to be happy
because that feeling is starting to fade from my memory

thank you

i laughed, i smiled, we talked
it was fun, it was good

opposite to what everyone said
it was going to be like

i felt confident, and i felt safe with you, in your arms
so i thank you for that
for making sex a fun experience,
for showing me what sex is supposed to be,
for showing me how sex is supposed to feel,
for showing me that sex can be fun and that i can enjoy
it

so this is a thank you to my first and a goodbye to my
obsession

the laugh

every time i go out with my friends
i'm never the one to get picked
i get talked over
and the few things i do say, people talk louder or they
laugh
and i never felt so out of place and awkward
all i wanna do is cry in the bathroom but i try not to

i have myself

i know we are starting to drift apart
and when something happens in my life,
you are not the first person i want to tell anymore
when i wanna go somewhere, i don't ask you to come
with me
i write what's happening in my life in my diary at night,
i go places myself, i do things by myself
because recently i realized i don't need you the way i
once did
i have myself
so if you are okay with drifting apart, then so am i

i like me?

i genuinely don't know what has happened to me
i feel confident
i fell on top of the world
like i don't give a fuck about other people and their opinion
like i am my own person and i do whatever i want to do
it's a feeling i never felt this much and often before
i like it
i like me
and i think,
i even like the way i look

when i read

when i read i am not myself
i am not sitting in my bed reading letters on a few
hundred pages
i am not me, in this world
i explore other planets, worlds, universes
i am a *fea* warrior, a revolutionist, rebell, princess, queen,
assassin
in another world
i feel everything, do everything i read about
i have fallen in love with the people i read about
i have cried for them
i have laughed with them
i have lived and experienced a hundred lives and stories

my happiness first

why can't i do stuff that makes me happy? why can't i
follow my dreams?
it's always "ooh" or "i didn't know you were into that
stuff"
i just want someone to be genuinely happy for me
to be there for me and understand me
and understand that sometimes i need to do stuff for
me
even if i hurt someone or disappoint someone
i need to come first
and that's something i recently learnt
because i can't be happy if i don't put my own happiness
first

once i leave

it is so hard to leave the place you grew up in
your comfort zone until you do
because once i get out, i wouldn't want to come back
when you're already out it becomes so damned easy to
keep staying away

and the thing is, i don't think i will ever look back
when i once leave, i'm gone because all i ever done is
relied on myself
i need to fix something, i fix it
"m hungry, i make something to eat
i need cloths, i buy it
is it something i don't know how to do it, i look it up
all i need is me, and i won't be returning
relying on someone else?
no, all i need is me and i won't even give it a second
thought

i really want someone to get me throughly

i really want someone to know what i been through and
genuinely understand
because they have been through it as well
not that i wish anything i've been through on anyone,
but i just want to know that i am not alone
that others get it, get me
get why i cry when someone yells at me
get why i am quiet when i am around a big group of
people
get me when all i do is smile
and get it if it's a fake or a real smile
just understand me throughly

"my person"

i miss you
a person i do not know yet
but i believe i will meet you someday
"my person"
you will stand in my corner with me
you will lay down in the middle of a road at three a.m.
with me
you will make me laugh when all i want to do is cry
we will be blacked out drunk together on multiple
occasions
i know you will be there for me whenever
i will be there for you whenever

have you seen grey's anatomy?
meredith always has a person she calls "my person"
and that is exactly what you will be to me
"my person"
even if we are hundreds of miles apart, you will always
have me, no matter what
and i will always have you, no matter what

things i don't say out loud

i think i am so broken i will never be whole again
the pieces that are left won't quite ever fit together again

i will always have these scars that no one can see,
this heaviness around my heart,
that make the beating uneven

these holes in my lungs that leave them empty
no matter how deep breaths i take

i cannot outlive days, i feel like dying
and at this point
i have been so damage i do not remember
me ever being
unbroken

and you can see it in my eyes
because i am not good at concealing it
not at all
because if you look in between the gold and the brown
in my eyes
it is there

in plain site
how i am always on the verge of breaking

i am barely surviving most days

i do not want to exist

i do not want to exist; i want to live
i want to tell my future grandchildren how
i lived life to the fullest
i want to tell them how many oopsies i have
i don't want "what if's" i want "oopsie's"
i want my life to be like the movies
i want so many crazy memories i barely can count them
i want to

l i v e

i want to live my life just how i want it
no rules
no "no's"
only yes's
only:

m o m e n t o u s

my father was the first guy to ever break my heart

i never had my first heartbreak by a boy my age
i had it by my father because he broke my heart
when he chose another family
when he chose another's daughter before his own
when he did everything i wanted to do with him
with someone else's child
he was more a sperm donate than a dad
and even if he chose them years ago, i still wonder why
my inner child wonders what she did wrong
why he never chose to stay and be her dad
what if she could do something different to make him
stay?
stay and not be violent
not yell
not hit

that little child wonders if that is what love is supposed
to be
kind and gentle one second
and screams and fights the next?
is that love, dad?

super heroes

i thought that parents were supposed to be a child's safe
space
a child's heroes
but my parents never were
they never showed me unconditionally love
everything were on conditions
i was a good kid if i did that or this
i could always be better and show others how good i
was raised
and never complain
never be a kid
never cry or be upset
because if i did those things then i wasn't a good kid
i was, in the way
too loud

so
i started to become
smaller
quieter
more pleasing
and i never had a super hero
because i never once was saved
i was the savior to my "super heroes"

i try my hardest not to remember you

even though i try my hardest to forget about that night,
to forget about how you made me feel,
to forget about you
i fail every time
because i somehow still buy that
grape ice-flavored vape
you tasted like,
just to remember you clearer

to remember a glimpse
of what your skin felt like against mine

to remember a glimpse
of what your lips tasted like

to remember a glimpse
of how your eyes were looked on mine

so i buy that grape ice-flavored vape you tasted like
because a little part of me
do not want to forget about that night

but i will try my hardest, i promise

i crave male attention

i crave male attention but at the same time i resent it
i crave male attention from guys at a bar
i crave male attention from guys on the street
because if i don't get cat called,
if guys at a bar or a club don't want me,
am i even pretty?

that is not the real male attention i want though,
but at the same time it is

because i cannot get it from the guys
i can see myself gatch feelings for

can a man even have feelings for me?
can a man genuinely love me?
want me?
it has never happened yet
not even once in my eighteen years

so i resent male attention in a way
the way i crave it the most
from a man that loves me and wants me for me

because it is scary
giving your heart to someone
and not knowing what they will do with it
especially if it is your first time giving it away

depression some times

i think there is something wrong with me
somedays i just cannot bring myself out of bed
i cannot talk to people it is too much
i am too much
so i rather not talk at all
because they wouldn't even get it

life of a introverted

i hate when people say "oh i could never be home for a whole day"
i do that
rather i love being home a whole day and doing absolutely nothing at all
just reading or watching a show or just sleeping
but i get judged for it though
so i never say that to people
that i rather be at home than hanging out with them

because when i do go out
i get so anxious
i get sweaty
i overthink things i do
my face gets red all the time
i don't even know how to act
or interact with people

so i stay at home to reload a social battery that always is low

a home that i cannot reach

when i look at the stars
i feel my lips turning into a smile
because when you look close enough
you can see even the smallest star
and when i look up at them
the stars
all my problems go away even just for a moment
everything feels fine
and i feel like it doesn't matter if i'm invisible
to most people or
if they don't appreciate me or my present
because when i look up at the night sky
i am seen by the moon and the stars
and i am at home

kid

i only wanted to be a kid,
just once
and now i feel guilty

fight before you leave, please?

not a single person has
fought for me to stay in their life
yet i fought every time before someone left
that destroys you truly
that absolutely ruined me

my tattoos

my tattoos on my skin
is my whole story
printed on me
until the day i am nothing more than bone and dirt
some are story's
some are quotes i live by
and some are things i went through
and if you get the privilege to know the meaning
behind every single one of them,
then you know me
inside out

did i mean the same for you that you
meant for me ?

in my story, you were a
whole chapter
a few times
but for you,
in your story
my name was barely mentioned

i want someone to make me feel okay

i want someone to make me feel okay about
eating until i cannot eat anymore
i want someone to make me feel okay about
all the scars on my body
i want someone to make me feel okay about
my trauma
i want someone to make me feel okay about
being
me

do you deserve to know her?

my world did not collapse without you
when you left
in fact
my world is pretty damned in tacked
so i don't know if i need you

you left me

you tried to come back like nothing happened
but this, me
the new me happened, and you do not know her
and to be honest, i do not think you deserve to
know her either

a dream

i spent half of my life trying to be someone else
someone thinner
someone extrovert
someone likeable
someone extraordinary

i even dream about being another person
and every day i wake up
disappointed
realizing that it was just
a dream

home

i think this is it
this is the place i have been searching for
waiting for
the place i have been longing for

a place to call home
not a building with four walls and a roof
no
no
a place i can breathe in
a place i can go to and the heaviness in my chest
gets just a little easier to bear

figure it out

i do not mind doing everything on my own
i do not mind not asking you for help
that just means i am independent, right?
i do not need anyone's help with things anyways
i figure it out
i always figure it out

autumn

my favorite season is neither spring nor winter, and definitely not summer
my favorite season is autumn, believe it or not
when it's hot but not hot as in "a hot summer day and all you want to do is go to the beach," no, because i don't like the beach or i didn't used to, now though, i don't really mind
but when the weather gets colder and the leaves turn red, yellow and orange i get this feeling
this sensational feeling almost euphoric
for me it does not matter if it's raining, foggy or storming outside
i will be in my room
wrapped in one or two or even sometimes three blankets
reading
or watching a good movie or series
but mostly reading to the sound of the rain
tons of books
i say autumn is my favorite season, and everyone looks at me like i'm crazy, and maybe i am but that is my truth
autumn is my season

i am still thankful for you

i do not really know how we became so close
but we did
and i am grateful for it
because
i don't think i would be the person i am today if i'd
never met you
you helped me express myself
and turn into the real me
the me i usually never show anyone
but i showed you
and now
now i show everyone
even now
when we don't speak anymore
i will forever be thankful for you
and that i met you

when my season comes

when autumn comes
i will be at home
i will be safe again
i will feel that warm and cozy feeling every day
i will sit among the fallen leaves like a small fallen angel
and look up at the empty trees and watch the stars
and i will hear the rain through my bedroom window
while i read

and this will be my season again

i recently discovered self-love

"you can't love someone else before you love yourself"

i didn't believe that until recently
when i actually started to like myself
im almost proud of whom i am
i feel everything so different now
so more genuinely and so much more overwhelming
like i may be able to love me

relationships

i do not know what a healthy relationship with food
looks like
i've never had one
and i think i never will either

tired of my own depression

i do not want to exist anymore
my lungs are barely able to fill themselves with air
i am just surviving at this point
but that is not enough, no
no
not anymore
i want to go on adventures
i want to fall in love
i want to have my first heartbreak
i want to live
because when my time comes
i want to know
that i lived my life
to the fullest

leola

i envy her
she talks like everyone matters
she looks at everyone like they have a spotlight right on
their faces
she talks with confidence
she walks with confidence
she has this spark in her eyes
that makes everyone stop what they're doing and stare
she has this smile that light up everyone's day

if i would have a role model
it would be her
this
this stranger i met just barley
a month ago

how my thoughts see the light of day

i like being able to talk about my artistic side,
my writing
that is how i express myself
feelings
emotions
that are tucked away on shelves i cannot reach
within myself
those
things
my thoughts
can only see the light of the day
when i say the words
in a poem
like this one
and every single one of them
is a part of me

head held high

she is herself through and through
and no one can put out that ember
no
that
f i r e
that fire that burns deep within her core
her bone marrow

and that fire grows bigger and bigger
within the hour
within the minute
within the second
so big that not even the biggest of waterfalls can put it
out

what i beg for

i beg to be able to enjoy life again
to be happy every hour of the day
not just when i am too occupied to think to really feel
everything
i beg to be able to breath
not shallow breaths but deep ones and feel everything
go away not just deep breaths to inhale smoke but fresh
air that fill my lungs and my body with stillness and
peace
i beg to be able to speak my thoughts
loud and clear
to everyone and not give a damn what they think of my
thoughts
i beg to be able to be myself
even in front of strangers or people i barely know
and be myself proudly
i beg myself to be able to say "fuck it, this is me! love it
or hate it, i don't give a fuck"

my definition of belonging

belonging is not a house nor a building
but a person
your soulmate
a puzzle piece that matches perfectly with your own
a match made in heaven
to prevent that feeling of loneliness
to have the comfort of knowing that your other half,
your real home is out there
somewhere
somewhere in the world

sad poetry

i sometimes wish people could look into my eyes and
see everything
see
me
how broken
how shattered i truly am
without me having to physically speak the words out
loud
i just wish that someone out there
could read me as clearly as you are reading this poem

love every part of me

love my strange mind
and my overthinking

love my insecurity
and my curiosity

love my chubbiness
and my appetite

please
love me truly and fully, every part, all of me
not just the parts you like
please
i will become the best version of myself
i promise
but i need you to love me

how i want to be loved

i want to be loved so badly, i can't even describe it
i want someone to hear me when i do not speak
i want someone to hug me
just because they can
i want someone to give me forehead kisses
just because they want to
i want someone to understand that
i sometimes do not know how to show my love other
than weird faces, poking them and annoy them
i want someone to know
that i do not know my own mind
nor what's going on in there
but
i will try my best to show my affection,
somehow

what i hope for

i hope to live,
not just survive

i hope to be happy and
healed from everything

i hope i someday can speak to
strangers
without screaming inside

i hope, that if i cannot find anyone
to dance in the rain with me
i will dance alone

i hope to see every corner in this world
i desire to see all of it

i hope i will be able
to see my reflection
and instead of resent it
i will admire it

i hope to be confident
in my own body and won't let my
body dysmorphia
keep me from living

i hope to fall in love
with myself
and the life i am living

colorful

they say "your not worth it"

and i say "you may not see it, not everyone does ether,
but i am worth the world and everything in it, all of it"

they look at me, with disappointment but mostly fear
and i look at them with pity, it must be boring, watching
the world through their eyes
and i think that they never will see the world like i do
colorful

alive

are you alive?

what makes you feel alive?

such a weird question, right?
i mean, we're all living creatures
the real question should be:
what makes you *want* to be alive?

for me, it would be to experience everything,
every goddamned feeling and being consumed by it
living
a few years ago, i was thinking "what would happen if i
just died?"
but now
now i've realized i do not wish to die without living first
without feeling alive

dear diary

i've realized that when i used to keep a diary,
when i was younger i only wrote in it when i was sad or
angry
but that is not what i want to look back at when i read
my diary in twenty five years or
that is not the only thing i would like to look back at
i want to look back in time and be able to experience all
of it again
not just the sad times
but the happy times,
or the "new" times when i moved,
or switched jobs,
or studied,
or when i traveled,
when i settled down,
brought my own dog,
maybe even if i ever got married,
had children, grandchildren,
i want to be able to look back at my writings and realize
that i did it
i finally lived,
and i got to experienced everything

heartache

my heart aches to experience love
my heart aches to fall in love and to be loved
to feel that kind of love that consumes you, that kind of
love that makes all the other feelings disappear
sadness,
happiness,
disgust,
curiosity,
angriness,
disappointment,
pleasure,
everything
every other feeling blur and all you feel is love
the kind of love you only see in movies or read about in
books
my heart aches for *that* kind of love

my other skin

i came back
and everything is the same
my room
the view outside my window
the empty feeling i get every time i get up for work
how am i supposed to function when i have finally
learnt how to live
i went after the world and lived
i lived like nothing mattered
i lived like i was the center of attention, everything
circulated around me
i finally learned how to be no one but myself
and now i'm back where time stopped
and i'm back in this other skin
the skin i finally escaped
and the only thing i can think of now is when i can
escape next

the "plan"

it is so goddamned scary getting old
like what the hell am i supposed to do for fifty years?

i mean, i can't remember yesterday

and i'm too scared to plan my tomorrow

so all i can do is live today

but i cannot live today forever

but it's too scary to *not* have a plan

to not know what your gonna do tomorrow

i was supposed to know it from the beginning

my plan

m y l i f e

but it seems like my beginning hasn't even started yet .

little things

i knew that when i had to repeat myself on multiple
occasions
that they weren't listening
and i could not make them hear me

head of time

i write the endings ahead of time
i know i do
because i know that they're unavoidable
sooner or later, the end always comes
and it's not the "to be continue" kind of end
it's the "you'll never see them again" kind of end
i just wish that for once someone would be down for
the ride
the fun parts but also the bad ones
through the parts we hate each other but yet we make
up

but the make up part never comes
the ending is inevitable
it's always around the corner so i rather it end sooner
than later
because i don't know how many more endings i can take
before i finally break
i rather it end before i know you
before i've learnt to care for you
before i'm attached to you
so please, if you won't stay till the end, then don't let
me know you at all

an alcoholic

i wouldn't say i'm an addict
i mean how can i be?
i don't drink everyday
and i've never even done drugs,
not willingly anyway
but i miss it
being drunk
smiling and laughing at everything
feeling like i'm on cloud nine
feeling confident
walking up to a stranger and immediately become
friends
wondering how the fuck i will get home, and just laugh
at it
i even like the getting ready part
almost as much
so maybe i am an addict
so call me an alcoholic for all i care
but that feeling
being drunk

i fucking love that feeling

sword fight

when i don't write i am not myself
because somehow that keeps my demons away
like a shield
protecting the person holding it from a sword
metal against metal
or like opening a window in a dark room

it's cleansing
it's healing
and yet somehow i feel broken by writing
because i see everything clearer
i see exactly how broken i am
i see every little shattered piece by my soul in a new light
and when i think i have seen all of them i find more
i know this world is cruel, but having one single human
go through all these things are
cruel,
brutal,
savage,
so i write
and try to survive a sword fight with one shield

sign of the times

you ruined one of my favorite songs for me
did you know that?
a perfectly good song
and for what?
a friendship we don't even acknowledge anymore
i'm trying to move on
and i think you've already forgotten my name
but i'm stuck wondering how you could just turn your
back
i mean, you didn't even look back
not once
how could our friendship mean so much to me but so
little to you?
that's why it will get so hard for me to trust new people
because of you
because of how you left
the way you stopped answering
from talking everyday
you stopped
and a little part of me stopped beating with you

i hate you

i hate you
i hate you
i completely and utterly hate you
with everything i own
with everything i do
i hate you
but somehow
you was the reason i started to get more piercings
the reason i got tattoos
because i do not want you to recognize me
i do not want you to have a picture of me in your wallet
i do not even want you to be proud of me
of who i've become
i didn't grew into this wonderful being thanks to you
nor because of you
i grew into this wonderful being despite you
and maybe by hating you i feel close to you in some
weird fucked up way
but you messed me up
first by not being present
then by being violent
and now your absent

your face is starting to blur
i don't know if your hair is completely gray now or just
patches of it
or if you have colored your hair black again
but your voice
that
that is long gone
it was the first thing my brain pushed over the edge,
into blackness
i don't even remember the way you yelled at me or how
your punches sounded like
so i am left with nothing but hatred
so if you ever see me again
just now, that is not your little girl anymore
and i don't think i ever was

my idea of a family

i think i have a fucked up idea of what a family are
because i am used to broken promises and absent father
figures and conditional love and bargens

and that is not what you see on tv

but maybe that's the only way you were able to love me
maybe you were to hurt too love any other way

and maybe i should just forgive and forget about my
heritage

but you didn't just leave us when you left

you burnt down the house when you closed the door
behind you

genuine friends, where are you?

i should really know this by now and learn from my
mistakes, but i give too much
i even go that extra mile for people who don't really
deserve it
i mean...
i would break myself apart just so someone would like
me,
and i don't know why, i just do that
all the time
and for once i would like to be someone's first call so
fucking much it hurts
it physically hurts to know for a fact that you're no one's
first call
but everytime it ends with me in tears alone in a ball
surrounded by strangers who wouldn't even care
i always choose the wrong or ungenuine friends, almost
like it's a dare
but please let me meet a stranger who gives and takes
equally
and not just drain me mentally
because right now, i am drained and it's not a battery i
can recharge with flattery on my own

a "for now" friend

i am the friend
your only friends with
until you find someone
better to be friends with
and that,
it's fucking
lonely

too much

i feel too fucking much

it's a blessing, yes
but mostly it's a curse

all my nineteen years i've lived
it has been a curse

i overthink
overfeel
and overreact

but i also
over care
over love
and overshare

someone that's too much
apparently

S.N

i think i may have found at least one or two friends
real ones though…

that may get me
and understands me
even when i am
quiet,
or weird
stupid
silly
ugly & too much
so now
i think i will do anything
to keep them in my life
something i thought i would never find

a thousand lives

i do not know why but it is something magical to
disappear into a new book getting to know all the
characters, the landscape and if it's fantasy, the order of
the world
like everything's possible
but mostly i get to live another life
i strongly believe that someone who reads gets to live a
thousand lives if you wish
because our human brain cannot separate a fictional
character from a real person
so we can easily escape this world into another just by
simply reading and let it consume us

extraordinary

i think i may be ruined, in the best way possible
my escape into books and strange worlds may be the
reason
because i can no longer see myself living an ordinary life
working an ordinary job
no
absolutely not
i want to live an extraordinary life inside a fantasy novel,
find an extraordinary love,
a soul mate perhaps
win battles
have magic or at least it would exist in the world
i do think i would ace at that,
a fantasy life
be genuinely happy
in an extraordinary world

warrior

i have lost count on how many times i wished i would
just drop dead
i was never a believer or faithful
but i used to beg to whatever god that would listen to
make it quick
please
because i could not bear another day
another sunrise
so every night i begged on my bare knees
because i could not do it myself
i used to think i was to weak,
i was too frail
even in my dreams i dreamed i was dead and i was
someone else
but now i don't see that as a cowardly act anymore
that sliver of
what if i could survive it, thought
now i see that as a warrior's thought inside a little girl's
mind, wanting her to hang on
just one more day
one more
you can handle another

until one morning that little girl had become the warrior
and that warrior loved waking up
loved seeing another sunrise
loved living
wishing not to exist was barely even a memory
she could no longer imagine herself dead
she imagined herself living and breathing deeply, in and
out again
repeat
breathe in, hold, breathe out
the warrior said to herself "can you feel that? air filling
your lungs with life"

"was it my fault?"

the girl looked at her own reflection and smiled
she liked her outfit
it was cute
shorts and a tank top
it was a hot summer day
happiness radiated from her body

when the girl got home,
she hid them in her closet
hoped no one would find them
and the short asked "was it my fault?"
"no, it happened when she wore me to"
said the skirt in the shadows
all the way in the back of her closet
and the girl never looked back

doomed

i think i am doomed to end up with someone who either
looks like or behaves like my father
unfortunately
that's a subconscious thing we humans tend to do
and for me...
that would mean to continue the cycle

weekends

i used to hate weekends
i had nothing to do
i hated being home
unless i was watching a tv show or played pc games or
reading
and to be honest i never had any good friends i could
do things with
but now
now i live for the weekends
or at least the three weekends i'm off work
because now i have great friends to catch up with
i can go out
i can even handle being alone now
something i never could before
i even love to be alone at home on the days i'm off work
to do stuff i want to do
to reload
for the next five days to come
to live on the weekends once again

move mountains

there is over seven billion people on this planet
this earth
and you will meet good ones
great even
but
they might not be good to you
you just got to find your kind of people
and when you do
holy fuck you'll be able to move mountains

i have time

actually, life is beautiful and i have time
i have time to make mistakes
i have time to be young

marathon

when i was fifteen, i never could imagine myself turning
twenty
ever
i feel so young still that adult life is chasing me
i sprint
but it's a marathon
and every time i look over my shoulder, another month
has passed by
i can't outrun it
the aging
it's so damned terrifying

gray

you took my youth from me the moment you put your
hand inside my pants
and i hate the way everyone around me says i'm mature
for my age
because i'm not
not by choice anyway
my childhood got stolen from me
and people ask me why i'm acting like i'm forty
and the answer is…
that the world turned grey that day,
and has been ever since

to the people you let touch your soul

some people come into your life not to stay but to be
with you for a season
a few chapters maybe

and i should be grateful for them
because every person that touched my soul
change
no, shape me
and teaching me something
every relationship i have leaves me with a lesson

to you who are reading this
every person you allow to touch your soul should be
grateful
because you are allowing them to shape a beautiful,
outstanding creature
YOU

gold brown & obsidian black

sometimes when i look in the mirror i don't even
recognize what looks back at me
i mean, i see glimpses in those earthy brown eyes
that i used to know
used to recognize
but i wouldn't say they're earth brown anymore
no
they're gold brown with a hint of obsidian black in them
because no matter what no one could break them
and no one could take away the life from them
they still have their spark

the lies i tell my mother

"why do you always need to wear those earbuds?"
my mother ask me
once
"i want to"
i answer her
"do you listen to music?"
my mother ask me
twice
"yes"
i answer
"it's not good for your ears to always have those in, you
know"
my mother said
a few times to me
"yeah, okay"
i answer
vaguely

those are the only answers i can give her
because i cannot give her the real ones
that music in my ears keeps my thoughts in cheek
that it keeps my demons away

that i do not like my own thoughts when it is quiet
that i don't *want* to listen to music all the time
but i *need* to
when my mind is full with music i can pick and choose
which thoughts make it to my head and which don't
or if i don't want to think at all

i don't like to lie to my mother but it's easier
no *real* questions asked
so
i am truly sorry, mom
for all the lies i have told you
but i think it's better this way
to keep my demons away from you
as well

new days to come

remember there's always another beautiful sunrise to
see
another day to welcome
new people to meet
new books to read
so there's never too late to start over
tomorrow
because
tomorrow is a new
beginning

something to someone

i've never actually been in a relationship
i mean, i've liked people
had crushes here and there
none of the things i felt were ever received
which is a damn shame
because i know
i would have loved them
unconditionally
with every piece of my heart
my soul
i would have all these cute date ideas
like
midnight picnic
stargazing
night swim
breakfasts in a little cafe
road-trips but none of us would know where we're
going
but it's turning into a whole adventure just trying to find
our way home again
walks in the rain
dancing in the rain

dancing three am in my refrigerator light
because we've been up all night watching movies

and i would remember all the little things
like
when you talk about something you love and how your
eyes lighten up and your smile becomes a lighthouse
if i ever would be lost
all i'll ever need is your smile to guide me back home
because your smile would be my home
you
would be home
and i would do almost anything to see that beautiful
smile of yours
and just breathe you in

but i've never had a *you* to come home to
i've never been *someone's*
i've never had a high school sweetheart
or a sweetheart in general
but i know
i would be a good partner
a good
something to someone

my way down

to you who helped me heal

to you who let me honest about how i am feeling or
how my day have been

to you who would let me cry all night in my car with
you beside me if i needed to

to you who make me laugh when i don't want to

to you who would go out of your way for me

to you who would walk at least one mile if not more for
me

to you who's there to fix my heart, you didn't break

if heaven doesn't want you
i will go to hell with you

the first friend to say goodbye before they leave

the first friend to have a "talk" before the friendship
either end or work through the tough part
i think that talk healed a lot more than the friendship
on my part
because you listen and tried to understand what i had to
say
and in return i did the same
we didn't get aggressive
or ignored each other

thank you for saying goodbye before you leave
or in this case
thank you for saying
"i actually value this friendship, so let us work through
this"
i appreciate you now more than ever